Complete Student Key for Reinforcement Exercises

Business English
10th Edition

Mary Ellen Guffey
Emerita Professor of Business
Los Angeles Pierce College

Carolyn M. Seefer
Professor of Business
Diablo Valley College

SOUTH-WESTERN
CENGAGE Learning

Australia • Brazil • Japan • Korea • Mexico • Singapore • Spain • United Kingdom • United States

SOUTH-WESTERN
CENGAGE Learning

© 2011, 2008 South-Western, Cengage Learning

ALL RIGHTS RESERVED. No part of this work covered by the copyright herein may be reproduced, transmitted, stored, or used in any form or by any means graphic, electronic, or mechanical, including but not limited to photocopying, recording, scanning, digitizing, taping, Web distribution, information networks, or information storage and retrieval systems, except as permitted under Section 107 or 108 of the 1976 United States Copyright Act, without the prior written permission of the publisher except as may be permitted by the license terms below.

For product information and technology assistance, contact us at
**Cengage Learning Academic Resource Center,
1-800-423-0563.**

For permission to use material from this text or product, submit all requests online at **www.cengage.com/permissions**.
Further permissions questions can be emailed to
permissionrequest@cengage.com.

ISBN-13: 978-0-538-75684-6
ISBN-10: 0-538-75684-5

South-Western Cengage Learning
5191 Natorp Boulevard
Mason, OH 45040
USA

Cengage Learning is a leading provider of customized learning solutions with office locations around the globe, including Singapore, the United Kingdom, Australia, Mexico, Brazil, and Japan. Locate your local office at: **international.cengage.com/region**.

Cengage Learning products are represented in Canada by Nelson Education, Ltd.

For your course and learning solutions, visit
www.cengage.com.

Purchase any of our products at your local college store or at our preferred online store
www.CengageBrain.com.

NOTE: UNDER NO CIRCUMSTANCES MAY THIS MATERIAL OR ANY PORTION THEREOF BE SOLD, LICENSED, AUCTIONED, OR OTHERWISE REDISTRIBUTED EXCEPT AS MAY BE PERMITTED BY THE LICENSE TERMS HEREIN.

READ IMPORTANT LICENSE INFORMATION

Dear Professor or Other Supplement Recipient:

Cengage Learning has provided you with this product (the "Supplement") for your review and, to the extent that you adopt the associated textbook for use in connection with your course (the "Course"), you and your students who purchase the textbook may use the Supplement as described below. Cengage Learning has established these use limitations in response to concerns raised by authors, professors, and other users regarding the pedagogical problems stemming from unlimited distribution of Supplements.

Cengage Learning hereby grants you a nontransferable license to use the Supplement in connection with the Course, subject to the following conditions. The Supplement is for your personal, noncommercial use only and may not be reproduced, posted electronically or distributed, except that portions of the Supplement may be provided to your students IN PRINT FORM ONLY in connection with your instruction of the Course, so long as such students are advised that they may not copy or distribute any portion of the Supplement to any third party. Test banks and other testing materials may be made available in the classroom and collected at the end of each class session, or posted electronically as described herein.

Any material posted electronically must be through a password-protected site, with all copy and download functionality disabled, and accessible solely by your students who have purchased the associated textbook for the Course. You may not sell, license, auction, or otherwise redistribute the Supplement in any form. We ask that you take reasonable steps to protect the Supplement from unauthorized use, reproduction, or distribution. Your use of the Supplement indicates your acceptance of the conditions set forth in this Agreement. If you do not accept these conditions, you must return the Supplement unused within 30 days of receipt.

All rights (including without limitation, copyrights, patents, and trade secrets) in the Supplement are and will remain the sole and exclusive property of Cengage Learning and/or its licensors. The Supplement is furnished by Cengage Learning on an "as is" basis without any warranties, express or implied. This Agreement will be governed by and construed pursuant to the laws of the State of New York, without regard to such State's conflict of law rules.

Thank you for your assistance in helping to safeguard the integrity of the content contained in this Supplement. We trust you find the Supplement a useful teaching tool.

Printed in the United States of America
2 3 4 5 6 7 8   14 13 12 11

Complete Student Key
Table of Contents

Answers to Reinforcement Exercises

Chapter 1 1

Chapter 2 2

Chapter 3 3

Chapter 4 5

Chapter 5 7

Chapter 6 9

Chapter 7 11

Chapter 8 13

Chapter 9 16

Chapter 10 18

Chapter 11 20

Chapter 12 23

Chapter 13 25

Chapter 14 28

Chapter 15 31

Chapter 16 33

Chapter 17 35

Chapter 18 37

Answers to Reinforcement Exercises

Chapter 1

Exercise B
1. b
2. c
3. a
4. b
5. d
6. a
7. c
8. a
9. a
10. b

Exercise C
1. coworker
2. inasmuch as
3. in-depth
4. online
5. out-of-date
6. workplace
7. first-class
8. first class
9. day care
10. Web site

Exercise D
1. com — equivalent, similar
2. des — an arid, barren tract
3. sert — to abandon
4. fat — untiring
5. rev — unalterable
6. post — occurring after death
7. be — of or relating to the Caribbean Sea
8. lec — relating to a voter or vote
9. mis — harmful, injurious
10. mer — an illusion

Exercise E
1. b
2. a
3. b
4. a
5. d
6. a
7. b
8. b
9. c
10. d

Exercise F
Answers will vary.

Complete Student Key

Chapter 2

Exercise B
1. verb
2. adjective
3. noun
4. adjective
5. noun
6. verb
7. noun
8. adjective
9. verb
10. noun

Exercise C
Answers will vary.

Exercise D
1. The—adjective (article)
2. e-mail—adjective
3. message—noun
4. contained—verb
5. virus—noun
6. but—conjunction
7. it—pronoun
8. was—verb
9. quickly—adverb
10. deleted—verb

1. Wow—interjection
2. She—pronoun
3. immediately—adverb
4. determined—verb
5. the—adjective (article)
6. cause—noun
7. of—preposition
8. company—adjective
9. network—adjective
10. problem—noun

Exercise E
1. offer—action
2. provides—action
3. selected—action
4. sounds—linking
5. deliver—action
6. studied—action
7. are—linking
8. felt—linking
9. dreams—action
10. am—linking

Exercise F
1. b
2. d
3. b
4. a
5. b
6. a
7. c
8. d
9. a
10. b

Exercise G
Answers will vary.

Chapter 3

Exercise B
1. b
2. a
3. b
4. a
5. d
6. b
7. d
8. b
9. b
10. b

Exercise C
1. D
2. I
3. I
4. D
5. P
6. D
7. I
8. P
9. D
10. P

Exercise D
1. simple
2. compound
3. simple
4. compound
5. complex
6. simple
7. complex
8. simple
9. complex
10. simple

Exercise E
Answers will vary.

Pattern 1: Subject—Verb
Answers will vary.
1. The football team—won
2. Our office—is moving
3. Students—study
4. Health costs—have increased
5. The committee—voted
6. E-mail messages—arrive

Pattern 2: Subject—Action Verb—Object
Answers will vary.
7. Licia answered the—telephone
8. FedEx delivers—packages
9. Salespeople sold—products
10. Congress passes—laws
11. Stock pays—dividends
12. Students threw a—party

Complete Student Key

Pattern 3: Subject—Linking Verb—Complement
Answers will vary.
Noun or pronoun complements
13. The applicant was—he *or* Michael
14. Chandra is the new—accountant
15. The caller could have been—she *or* Kathy
16. The president is—he *or* Ms. Jones

Adjective complements
17. My investment was—profitable
18. New York is—exciting
19. Our new supervisor is—friendly
20. The report could have been—longer

Exercise F
1. a
2. c
3. d
4. b
5. a
6. d
7. c
8. b
9. a
10. b

Exercise G
1. a.
2. c
3. d
4. b
5. a
6. b
7. b
8. d
9. c
10. a

Exercise H
Answers will vary.
1. Because I am looking for a position in hotel management, I am interested in your job posting.
2. We are seeking a management trainee who has not only good communication skills but also computer expertise.
3. During job interviews candidates must provide details about their accomplishments, which is why they should rehearse answers to expected questions.
4. Although an interviewer will typically start with general questions about your background, be careful to respond with a brief history.
5. A candidate who provided a wide range of brief stories about specific accomplishments was hired.

Exercise I
1. b
2. b
3. a
4. b
5. b
6. a
7. a
8. a
9. a
10. c

Complete Student Key

Exercise J
Answers will vary.

Chapter 4

LEVEL 1
Exercise B
1. b
2. a
3. c
4. b
5. a
6. b
7. b
8. a
9. a
10. c

Exercise C
1. employees
2. lice
3. watches
4. witnesses
5. franchises
6. quotas
7. lunches
8. feet
9. glasses
10. marshes
11. waltzes
12. hunches
13. geese
14. biases
15. glitches
16. services
17. gases
18. women
19. committees
20. oxen

Exercise D
1. C
2. A
3. C
4. C
5. A
6. A
7. C
8. A
9. C
10. A

LEVEL 2
Exercise B
1. b
2. c
3. a
4. b
5. c
6. b
7. b
8. a
9. b
10. a
11. b
12. b
13. a
14. c
15. b
16. b
17. a
18. c
19. b
20. c

Complete Student Key

Exercise C
1. balances of trade
2. halves
3. bills of sale
4. IPOs
5. subsidiaries
6. M's
7. Wednesdays
8. liabilities
9. Sanchezes
10. valleys
11. know-it-alls
12. ATMs
13. Cs
14. Nos.
15. governors-elect
16. ifs
17. logos
18. ft.
19. depts.
20. q's

Exercise D
Answers will vary.
1. Have the Alvarezes been invited?
2. Many standbys (not *standbies*) waited to get on the crowded flight.
3. Most loan officers know the dos and don'ts of credit.
4. She handles the portfolios for several clients.
5. Many ordinary heroes live among us.
6. The defense plans to call five witnesses to the stand.
7. Both attorneys were well prepared.
8. People with strong beliefs are more likely to become leaders.

LEVEL 3
Exercise B
1. b
2. c
3. a
4. a
5. b
6. a
7. c
8. a
9. b
10. a

Exercise C
1. a
2. c
3. b
4. b
5. c
6. a
7. a
8. c
9. b
10. c
11. a
12. b
13. a
14. b
15. c
16. b
17. c
18. c
19. c
20. a

Exercise D
1. teeth
2. wolves
3. electronics
4. ATMs
5. A's
6. inquiries
7. stimuli
8. taxes
9. women
10. potatoes
11. MDs
12. earnings
13. brushes
14. Ruizes
15. batches
16. employees
17. pros
18. portfolios
19. brothers-in-law
20. W-2s

Exercise E
1. b
2. a
3. b
4. a
5. b
6. a
7. b
8. c
9. b
10. c

Chapter 5

LEVEL 1
Exercise B
1. the job applicant's qualifications
2. the students' presentations
3. a seller's permit
4. patients' rights
5. customers' addresses
6. the organization's Web site
7. competitors' prices
8. Asians' buying power
9. several doctors' offices
10. stockholders' meeting

Exercise C
1. students'
2. employees'
3. company's
4. economists'
5. customers'
6. inventor's
7. passengers'
8. boss's
9. governor's
10. waitresses'

Exercise D
1. citizens'
2. boss's
3. witness's
4. Passengers'
5. employees
6. companies'
7. waitress's
8. companies
9. companies'
10. rates
11. client's
12. individual's
13. customers'
14. depositors

Complete Student Key

15. children's
16. taxpayers'
17. subscribers
18. athletes'
19. America's
20. chefs

LEVEL 2
Exercise B
1. States
2. graphics
3. staff's
4. Hemingway's
5. beneficiaries'
6. IRS's
7. avionics
8. NBC's
9. employees'
10. news
11. Norris's
12. company's
13. Inc.'s
14. ICC's
15. Fox's
16. attorney's
17. Ltd.'s
18. Microsoft's
19. claims
20. Tess's

Exercise C
1. The hourly fee of my sister's lawyer is high.
2. The support of Michael Jordan's father was instrumental to the athlete's success.
3. The success of Stephenie Meyer's latest book has been overwhelming.
4. The computer of the engineer's assistant held all the necessary equations.
5. The motor home of my supervisor's friend is always parked in the company lot.

LEVEL 3
Exercise B
1. Sue
2. company's
3. buyers'
4. Thomases'
5. week's
6. master's
7. dollar's
8. years'
9. people's
10. Attorneys'

Exercise C
1. Domino's
2. bachelor's
3. students
4. boss's
5. guests'
6. artists'
7. parties'
8. men's
9. CPAs'
10. employees'
11. father-in-law's
12. cents'
13. Jason's
14. HMO's
15. other's
16. DNA's
17. employees
18. eyewitnesses'
19. waitress's
20. Charlie's

Exercise D
1. a
2. b
3. b
4. c
5. c
6. a
7. b
8. a
9. a
10. b

Exercise E
Answers will vary.
1. Leonard's photographs were published in a national magazine.
2. The contractor's bid was too high.
3. Milli and Robert's honeymoon trip was a gift from their parents.
4. Some of Congress's latest laws may not withstand judicial review.
5. All customers' tips are divided among the servers and support staff.
6. Her mother-in-law's home was within walking distance.

Chapter 6

LEVEL 1
Exercise B
Answers will vary.

Subjects	*Objects*
1. I	1. me
2. we	2. us
3. he	3. him
4. she	4. her
5. they	5. them

Exercise C
1. a
2. c
3. a
4. a
5. b
6. b
7. c
8. c
9. c
10. b
11. a
12. c
13. a
14. a
15. c
16. b
17. a
18. c
19. a
20. b

Exercise D
1. its
2. me
3. her
4. him
5. it's
6. me

7. theirs
8. them
9. Your
10. Ours

LEVEL 2
Exercise B
1. me
2. I
3. I
4. us
5. him
6. himself
7. we
8. he
9. he
10. him
11. I
12. I
13. me
14. me
15. us
16. he
17. us
18. her
19. her
20. him

Exercise C
1. he
2. me
3. he
4. her
5. me
6. its
7. he
8. we
9. your
10. her
11. me
12. theirs
13. hers
14. she
15. its
16. it's
17. us
18. You're
19. she
20. yours

Exercise D
Answers will vary.
1. My supervisor and I will attend the developers' conference in Dallas.
2. The two sales reps, Paul and he, broke the company sales record.
3. Just between you and me, will the manager be replaced?
4. Except for Yumiko and me, everyone has gone home.
5. The manager expected Jeff and me to work late whenever necessary.
6. The building and its contents were destroyed by fire.
7. Ours is the only office without its own parking spaces.

LEVEL 3
Exercise B
1. I
2. he
3. me
4. she
5. they
6. him and her
7. he
8. she
9. he
10. he

11. her
12. her
13. they
14. he
15. him
16. they
17. him
18. he
19. she
20. she

Exercise C
1. attorneys
2. its
3. Sally's
4. he
5. graphics
6. you're
7. I
8. it's
9. There's
10. employees
11. I
12. months'
13. I
14. us
15. company's
16. managers
17. We
18. I
19. RSVPs
20. she

Exercise D
1. b
2. b
3. a
4. b
5. c
6. b
7. b
8. a
9. a
10. c

Chapter 7

LEVEL 1
Exercise B
1. their
2. his or her
3. his or her
4. their
5. his
6. patients
7. he or she has
8. their
9. he or she
10. his or her

Exercise C
Answers will vary.
1. a. All new teachers must have their lesson plans approved.
   b. Every new teacher must have all lesson plans approved.
   c. Every new teacher must have his or her lesson plans approved.

2. a. Be sure that all new employees have received their orientation packets.
   b. Be sure that each new employee has received an orientation packet.
   c. Be sure that each new employee has received his or her orientation packet.

3. a. Doctors must submit their insurance paperwork on time.
   b. A doctor must submit all insurance paperwork on time.
   c. A doctor must submit his or her insurance paperwork on time.

Exercise D
Answers will vary.
1. The article reported that Google had acquired Image America and that Google planned to use Image America's aerial photography technology.
2. The management makes customers wear shirts and ties in that restaurant.
3. Mr. Williams told Mr. Whitman that Mr. Whitman needed to take a vacation.
4. Recruiters like to see job objectives on résumés; however, such objectives may restrict job candidates' chances.
5. Ms. Hartman talked with Courtney about Courtney's telecommuting request, but Ms. Hartman needed more information.

LEVEL 2
Exercise B
1. its
2. his or her
3. its
4. his or her
5. his or her
6. its
7. its
8. its
9. its
10. his or her
11. their
12. its
13. its
14. his or her
15. him or her

LEVEL 3
Exercise B
1. who
2. whoever
3. who
4. who
5. Whom
6. whom
7. whoever
8. whom
9. who
10. whomever
11. who
12. who
13. whoever
14. whom
15. whom
16. who
17. whom
18. whom
19. who
20. who

Exercise C
1. Who's
2. Who's
3. Whose
4. Who's
5. Whose
6. whose
7. who's
8. whose
9. Whose
10. Who's

Exercise D

1. its
2. its
3. their
4. his or her
5. its
6. its
7. whom
8. whoever
9. his
10. Whom
11. its
12. her
13. Who's
14. its
15. who
16. whoever
17. its
18. his or her
19. their
20. whose

Exercise E

1. a
2. b
3. c
4. b
5. a
6. b
7. c
8. b
9. a
10. b

Chapter 8

LEVEL 1
Exercise B

1. T (site)
2. I
3. T (packages)
4. T (prices)
5. I
6. I
7. T (messages)
8. I
9. I
10. I

Exercise C

1. is—famous
2. was—persuasive
3. smell—fantastic
4. sounds—resonant
5. was—she
6. was—photographer
7. feels—comfortable
8. appears—knowledgeable
9. sounds—feasible
10. seems—cold

Exercise D

1. L (Donna Holts)
2. T (image)
3. I
4. L (surprised)
5. L (she)
6. T (links)
7. T (employees)
8. L (accurate)
9. L (marvelous)
10. T (goods)
11. T (donation)
12. L (bright)
13. L (person)
14. T (effect)
15. T (service)
16. T (malware)
17. T (prescription)
18. I
19. L (bad)
20. L (interested)

LEVEL 2
Exercise B

1. active
2. active
3. passive
4. active
5. passive
6. active
7. active
8. passive
9. passive
10. active

Exercise C

Answers will vary.
1. General Motors greatly reduced pollution when it built its new plant.
2. Toyota designed a car with solar panels that will power the air conditioning system.
3. Filipinos send approximately one bill text messages every day.
4. Nike uses massive short-term financing to pay off its production costs during its slow season.
5. Insurance companies offer doctors cash rewards for prescribing generic drugs.
6. Investigators carefully reviewed the documents during the audit.
7. The webmaster recently redesigned our Web site to increase its attractiveness and effectiveness.
8. You must carefully calculate net income before taxes when you fill out your tax return.
9. The author detected only a few of the many errors and changes during the first proofreading.
10. AT&T constructed a cell phone tower in their neighborhood.

Exercise D

1. were
2. be
3. be
4. were
5. be
6. were
7. were
8. be
9. were
10. was

Exercise E
Answers will vary.
1. I wish that I were able to pilot an airplane.
2. If my boss were more understanding, I would have better hours.
3. If you were in my position, you would show more compassion.
4. She acts as if she were the Queen of England.
5. If he was at today's meeting, I didn't see him.

LEVEL 3
Exercise B
1. CEO's
2. Sandra's
3. his
4. Your
5. your
6. their
7. customer
8. their
9. player
10. His

Exercise C
1. b
2. a
3. b
4. b
5. a
6. a
7. b
8. a
9. a
10. b

Exercise D
Answers will vary.
1. When I have some free time, I would like to write a novel.
2. Because the company is doing well, I plan to buy some of its stock.
3. We were surprised by Arianna's quitting so suddenly.
4. When my visa is issued, I plan to work in Japan for a year.
5. If you haven't changed your mind, be sure to call to make your plane reservations.
6. Please inform your two agents that I appreciate their booking my reservation.
7. When you travel globally, try to ask good questions abut the culture before you leave.
8. Kent's service on the board has led to many corporate innovations.
9. Check to see whether the Web site is functioning properly.
10. Serona Software requires employees to spend an hour networking on Facebook every Friday.

Exercise E
Answers will vary.
1. Driving to the sales meeting, he turned the radio to NPR.
2. To be binding, every contract must be supported by a consideration.
3. As a baboon growing up in the jungle, Kiki, I realized, had special nutritional needs.
4. Selected as Employee of the Year, Cecile Change was presented an award by the CEO.
5. After breaking into the building, the burglars set off an alarm heard by the police.
6. An autopsy by the coroner revealed the cause of death to be strangulation.

7. A woman said someone stole a necklace, which was valued at worth $3,000, from a safe in her closet.
8. The man facing five counts of first-degree murder pleaded guilty while standing before the judge.
9. Dave Evola found his wallet lying under the front seat of his car.
10. From a helicopter, geologists inspected the site where the boulders broke free.

Exercise F
1. a
2. b
3. a
4. b
5. a
6. a
7. a
8. b
9. b
10. a

Chapter 9

LEVEL 1
Exercise B
1. opened, opens, will open
2. copied, copies, will copy
3. hurried, hurries, will hurry
4. tried, tries, will try
5. covered, covers, will cover
6. labeled, labels, will label
7. planned, plans, will plan
8. invested, invests, will invest
9. preferred, prefer, will prefer
10. sampled, sample, will sample

Exercise C
Answers will vary.
1. Ned flies to New York monthly to meet with clients.
2. Martha applied for a grant to study adult learning behaviors.
3. He will study until he passes the examination at a satisfactory level.
4. She learns new computer programs quickly.
5. Several companies canceled their travel plans.
6. The company will change to meet growing customer demands.
7. Madeline buys fresh produce daily.
8. General Motors trimmed 20 percent from its operating budget.
9. We will enclose our current catalog.
10. He stirred his coffee while reading the newspaper.

LEVEL 2
Exercise B
1. b
2. a
3. a
4. b
5. a
6. b
7. a
8. a
9. b
10. b

Exercise C
1. chosen
2. shrunk
3. bought
4. sunk
5. become
6. stole
7. taken
8. thrown
9. paid
10. led
11. fought
12. rung
13. brought
14. blew
15. thrown

Exercise D

Present	Past	Past Participle	Present Participle
lie (to rest)	lay	lain	lying
lay (to place)	laid	laid	laying

1. lie
2. lie
3. laid
4. lying
5. lain
6. lie
7. lay
8. lay
9. lying
10. laying

Exercise E

Present	Past	Past Participle	Present Participle
sit (to rest)	sat	sat	sitting
set (to place)	set	set	setting
rise (to go up)	rose	risen	rising
raise (to lift)	raised	raised	raising

1. raise
2. sit
3. raise
4. rises
5. setting
6. rising
7. raised
8. set
9. sits
10. risen

Exercise F
Answers will vary.

Complete Student Key

LEVEL 3
Exercise B
1. have learned
2. are anticipating
3. had done
4. was getting
5. will have opened
6. is thinking
7. have received
8. had finished
9. will be interviewing
10. will have arrived

Exercise C
1. b
2. a
3. c
4. a
5. b
6. a
7. b
8. c
9. a
10. b
11. a
12. a
13. b
14. b
15. a
16. b
17. c
18. b
19. b
20. a

Exercise D
1. a
2. b
3. a
4. b
5. b
6. b
7. b
8. a
9. a
10. b

Chapter 10

LEVEL 1
Exercise B
1. directory
2. administrator
3. services
4. cost, markup
5. one
6. emphasis
7. Farkas, Evans, & Everett, Inc.
8. anger, frustration
9. actor
10. time, money

Exercise C
1. a
2. a
3. a
4. b
5. a
6. a
7. b
8. a
9. a
10. b

Exercise D

1.	a	11.	a
2.	a	12.	b
3.	a	13.	a
4.	a	14.	b
5.	a	15.	b
6.	b	16.	b
7.	b	17.	a
8.	a	18.	a
9.	a	19.	a
10.	b	20.	b

LEVEL 2
Exercise B

1.	b	11.	a
2.	a	12.	a
3.	b	13.	b
4.	b	14.	b
5.	b	15.	a
6.	a	16.	b
7.	b	17.	a
8.	b	18.	a
9.	a	19.	b
10.	b	20.	a

Exercise C
Answers will vary.
1. The staff is recommending that a flexible workweek be implemented.
2. The staff are raising their hands to vote on the issue.
3. Our city council has recently voted to restrict spending.
4. Not one of the plans was acceptable to the committee.
5. Some of the jury members believe that the prosecution's evidence is not relevant.
6. Some of the proposal needs to be rewritten.
7. Somebody in the theater filled with patrons was using a cell phone.
8. Either Anne or you are responsible for locking up.
9. Either you or Anne was responsible for locking up.
10. Everything about the speeches was inspiring.

LEVEL 3
Exercise B

1.	a	6.	b
2.	b	7.	b
3.	b	8.	a
4.	a	9.	b
5.	a	10.	b

11. b
12. a
13. a
14. b
15. a
16. b
17. a
18. a
19. b
20. a

Exercise C
Answers will vary.
1. The most important traits I have to offer an employer are energy and enthusiasm.
2. The best parts of my job are preparing and analyzing financial statements.
3. The principal tasks in this office are abstracts and affidavits.
4. The primary reasons for his wealth are wise stock and other investment choices.
5. The main objectives this year are to increase sales and decrease expenses.
6. A number of businesses in our city are experiencing record profits.
7. The number of businesses that outsource is growing.
8. Every one of the students is studying hard for the exam.
9. Some of the employees are planning a retreat during the summer.
10. Some of the plan needs to be discussed in more detail.

Exercise D
1. There are
2. is
3. has
4. cause
5. Were
6. its
7. were
8. Is
9. are
10. are
11. is
12. seems
13. are
14. is
15. surrounds
16. is
17. has
18. strive
19. has
20. Every one

Exercise E
1. a
2. b
3. c
4. a
5. a
6. b
7. a
8. b
9. b
10. a

Chapter 11

LEVEL 1
Exercise B
1. b
2. b
3. b
4. a
5. b
6. b
7. a
8. a

9. b
10. b
11. b
12. a
13. b
14. a
15. a
16. a
17. b
18. b
19. b
20. b

Exercise C
1. most (least) creative
2. better
3. most (least) current
4. easier
5. more (less) quiet *or* quieter
6. least
7. more (less) professional
8. kinder
9. worst
10. more (less) interesting

LEVEL 2
Exercise B
1. a
2. b
3. a
4. b
5. b
6. b
7. b
8. b
9. b
10. a
11. b
12. b
13. b
14. a
15. b
16. a
17. a
18. b
19. b
20. a

Exercise C
1. a
2. an
3. an
4. a
5. a
6. a
7. an
8. an
9. an
10. a
11. an
12. an
13. an
14. a
15. an

Exercise D
1. b
2. a
3. b
4. a
5. a
6. a
7. b
8. a
9. a
10. a
11. a
12. b
13. a
14. a

Complete Student Key

15. b
16. b
17. b
18. a
19. a
20. b

Exercise E
1. yellow sports car
2. honest, fair appraisal
3. concise, courteous e-mail message
4. innovative software program
5. direct, practical approach
6. snug, cheerful apartment
7. imaginative, daring designer
8. skilled financial analyst
9. impractical budget item
10. rising stock prices

Exercise F
Answers will vary.
1. Our health care provider increased fees.
2. He bought a first-class ticket to Shanghai.
3. She was offered a part-time position.
4. Our two-year-old equipment already needs upgrading.
5. This is a once-in-a-lifetime opportunity.
6. Please follow the month-by-month plan.
7. Only work-related expenses are reimbursed.
8. Their latest model represents state-of-the-art technology.
9. I left you a voice mail message.
10. The day care center has special hours on weekends.

LEVEL 3
Exercise B
1. a
2. b
3. a
4. a
5. b
6. b
7. a
8. b
9. a
10. b
11. a
12. b
13. b
14. a
15. b
16. b
17. a
18. b
19. a
20. a

Exercise C
Answers will vary.
1. How much farther is the gas station?

2. She is returning to school to further her education.
3. In comparing paperbound and hardbound books, I prefer the latter.
4. Fewer accidents were reported for this holiday than in previous years.
5. Less preparation is needed for entry-level jobs.

Exercise D
1. b
2. a
3. a
4. b
5. a
6. a
7. b
8. a
9. b
10. b

Exercise E
1. a
2. b
3. b
4. a
5. b
6. a
7. b
8. b
9. a
10. a

Chapter 12
LEVEL 1
Exercise B
1. b
2. a
3. b
4. a
5. b
6. b
7. b
8. a
9. a
10. b
11. b
12. a
13. b
14. b
15. a
16. b
17. b
18. b
19. a
20. b

LEVEL 2
Exercise B
1. Where should I send the application form?
2. A new café is opening opposite the park.
3. Special printing jobs must be done outside the office.
4. Charles had great respect for and interest in the stock market.
5. Who can tell me what time the meeting is scheduled?
6. What style of clothes is recommended for the formal dinner?
7. Leah couldn't help laughing when Noah spilled his latte as he walked into the conference room.
8. Where shall we move the extra desks and chairs?

9. Lee Montgomery graduated from college with a degree in graphic design.
10. What type of return policy does Zappos.com have?
11. Please write her performance appraisal quickly.
12. Our appreciation for and interest in the program remain strong.
13. When did you graduate from college?
14. Where do you live?
15. I didn't mean to wake you.

Exercise C

1.	a	11.	a
2.	b	12.	a
3.	b	13.	a
4.	b	14.	a
5.	a	15.	b
6.	a	16.	b
7.	a	17.	b
8.	b	18.	b
9.	a	19.	a
10.	b	20.	b

Exercise D
1. To whom did you send payment?
2. Please locate the file in which you put the contract.
3. With what companies did you apply?
4. We have a number of loyal members upon whom we can rely.
5. From what company did you purchase these supplies?

LEVEL 3
Exercise B

1.	b	11.	b
2.	a	12.	a
3.	a	13.	b
4.	b	14.	b
5.	a	15.	a
6.	b	16.	a
7.	b	17.	b
8.	b	18.	a
9.	a	19.	b
10.	a	20.	a

Exercise C
Answers will vary.
1. Working at her computer, Christie was oblivious to the chaos around here.
2. Cary often finds it difficult to reconcile the company checkbook with the bank statement.
3. Kelly is reconciled to the fact that her sister will always earn more than she does.

4. I plan to apply to graduate schools.
5. The model we received differs from the model we ordered online.

Exercise D
1. a
2. b
3. b
4. a
5. a
6. c
7. a
8. b
9. b
10. a

Chapter 13

LEVEL 1
Exercise B
1. a
2. b
3. b
4. b
5. a
6. a
7. b
8. a
9. b
10. b

Exercise C
1. confidential,
2. Correct
3. *bull markets*,
4. Correct
5. employees,
6. theft; however,
7. learn, however,
8. faced, nevertheless,
9. problem;
10. 1963; consequently,

Exercise D
Answers will vary.
1. Morgan studied hard for his accounting exam, and he earned the highest grade in the class.
2. Brooke enjoys hiking, wakeboarding, and cycling.
3. She is considering a career in public relations or journalism.
4. Sales are increasing dramatically; consequently, we will hire three additional salespeople.
5. We think, consequently, that we will need three new desks and computers.
6. This year we hired only one new employee, but next year we hope to add several more.
7. Our competitor is advertising heavily; nevertheless, we see little change in our share of the market.
8. We are convinced, nevertheless, that we need additional advertising support.
9. Survey employees about their preferences; then tabulate the results.
10. We are not sure, however, that the candidate is qualified for the position.

LEVEL 2
Exercise B
1. b
2. c
3. a
4. b
5. a
6. c
7. b
8. a
9. a
10. a

Exercise C

Coordinating Conjunctions	Conjunctive Adverbs	Subordinating Conjunctions
and	however	if
but	moreover	although
yet	consequently	because
nor	thus	since
or	then	when

Exercise D
1. b
2. a
3. a
4. b
5. a
6. b
7. a
8. b
9. a
10. b
11. a
12. b
13. a
14. a
15. b
16. b
17. a
18. b
19. a
20. b

Exercise E
Answers will vary.
1. If you like my ideas, please vote to adopt them.
2. Please call me if you have any questions.
3. Because so many of our employees telecommute, we are purchasing additional wireless devices.
4. Brittany plans to join the Sierra Club because she believes in its mission.
5. Although most people today own a cell phone, many complain that other cell phone users are rude.
6. After I complete my degree, I will look for a permanent job.
7. Taxpayers who donate to charity will get tax breaks.
8. Bob Mensch, who donated to charity, received a tax break.
9. The idea that was adopted came from a group of students.
10. LL Bean, which is located in Maine, still sells predominantly through its mail-order catalog.

LEVEL 3
Exercise B
1. a
2. a
3. b
4. b
5. a
6. b
7. b
8. a
9. b
10. b

Exercise C
Answers will vary.
1. Stocks can be purchased either online or from a broker.
2. Neither the staff nor the students were happy with the proposed cutbacks in class offerings.
3. The Small Business Administration not only provides training but also guarantees loans.
4. Because users of cell phones are often guilty of boorish behavior, many restaurants and other public places have imposed bans. *OR:* Users of cell phones are often guilty of boorish behavior; therefore, many restaurants and other public places have imposed bans.
5. Because old computer hardware creates hazardous dump sites, computer manufacturers are starting recycling programs. *OR:* Old computer hardware creates hazardous dump sites; therefore, manufacturers are starting recycling programs.

Exercise D
Answers will vary.
1. Rusty, who was recently hired as a transportation engineer, will work for Werner Enterprises, which is located in Omaha, Nebraska.
2. While teaching English to German employees of HSBC, Marlon Lodge, who is a British linguist and musician, discovered that his students caught on more quickly when he set new vocabulary to music.
3. Japanese ranchers, who learned that cows respond to beeps, equipped their herds with pagers; consequently, these ranchers need fewer workers.
4. Before sitting down at their computers, skilled writers save time for themselves and for their readers by organizing their ideas into logical patterns.
5. Nancy Burnett, who is a single parent with merchandising experience, started a mall-based chain of stores that sell fashionable, durable children's clothing.

Exercise E
1. b
2. c
3. a
4. a
5. b
6. b
7. b
8. a
9. a
10. b

Chapter 14

LEVEL 1
Exercise B
1. date, time zone — January 1, 1908, at 12 a.m.,
2. geographical item — Detroit,
3. C—essential appositive
4. series — bigger, better, faster,
5. parenthetical — say, consequently,
6. direct address — us, Mr. Trump,
7. series — Gillette, Norwegian Cruise Line, Arby's,
8. parenthetical — fact,
9. address — Department, 149 South Barrington Avenue, Los Angeles, CA 90049,
10. nonessential appositive — Walton, the founder of Wal-Mart,
11. date — July 28, 2005,
12. parenthetical — opened, of course,
13. parenthetical — Nevertheless,
14. series — Hawaii, Mexico,
15. C—one-word appositive
16. series — Phone, cable,
17. parenthetical — needed, however,
18. C—essential appositive
19. nonessential appositive — Darrow, who was a heater salesman in Pennsylvania,
20. time zone — 8 p.m.,

Exercise C
1. (2) Matt, Susan,
2. (2) Matt, a journalist for a U.S. newspaper,
3. C
4. (4) dancing, loud music, kissing, holding hands,
5. C
6. (4) hope, Mark,   Hannibal, Missouri,
7. (5) Florida, Missouri, on Sunday, November 30, 1835,
8. (2) apprentice,   pilot,
9. (3) Washington,   officer,   1:30 a.m.,
10. (1) Friday,
11. (4) Verrett, 160 Tolman Drive, Philadelphia, Pennsylvania 19106,
12. (2) letter, of course,
13. (3) meantime,   facts, testimonials,
14. (5) Incidentally,   Dallas, Texas, and Charleston, South Carolina,
15. (3) martial arts, Pilates, aqua fitness,
16. (2) Western Air Express, a former U.S. Airline,
17. (4) analysis, Mr. and Mrs. Parker,   2008, 2009,
18. (2) people, by the way,

19. (4) Administration,   2003,   start, manage,
20. C

LEVEL 2
Exercise B
1. short prepositional phrase — C
2. independent clauses — Fair,
3. nonessential clause — PictureTel, a subsidiary of IBM,
4. short prepositional phrase — C
5. independent adjectives — reliable,
6. introductory verbal phrase — leader,
7. introductory clause — you,
8. introductory clause — dictionary,
9. nonessential clause — Bricklin,   spreadsheet,
10. essential clause — C
11. introductory clause — loans,
12. terminal clause — C
13. independent clauses — considered,
14. nonessential paren. clause — salaries, as you might have expected,
15. long intro. prep. phrase — months,
16. short prepositional phrase — C
17. introductory verbal phrase — desk,
18. independent adjectives — overpaid,
19. nonessential clause — Cohen,   Jerry's,
20. introductory verbal phrase — 2005,

Exercise C
1. (1) seamless,
2. (1) daily,
3. (2) Enfield, a north London suburb,
4. (1) correct,
5. (2) insurance,   April 1,
6. (2) happy,   examinations,
7. (1) chair,
8. (1) peppy,
9. (1) year,
10. (2) Perez,   Eastman Kodak,
11. (1) systems,
12. C
13. (1) sales,
14. (1) inefficient
15. (1) message,
16. (2) predicted, the resourceful,
17. C
18. (2) rates,   adequate,

Complete Student Key

19. (1) speeding,
20. (3) Safeco,   company,   Teensurance,

LEVEL 3
Exercise B
1. short quotation   world," said Mark Twain,
2. C
3. contrasting statement   confident,
4. short quotation   work,"
5. adjacent numerals, numerals 2009, 7,500
6. C
7. abbreviations   Craig, LVN,   Parrisher, RN,
8. clarity   paper,
9. contrasting statement   customers,
10. omitted words   secondary responsibility,
11. contrasting statement   stable, not risky,
12. short quotation   said,
13. clarity   short,
14. abbreviations   Meyer, PhD,   Massaglia, MD,
15. adjacent numerals, numerals 2008, 1,040,000
16. contrasting statement   General Motors Corp., not Ford Motor Co.
17. omitted words   Ford Motor Co.,
18. clarity   What it was,
19. short quotation   greedy," said Warren Buffett,
20. C

Exercise C
Answers will vary.
1. Series. Available entrees include filet mignon, baked chicken, and vegetarian pasta.
2. Parenthetical. All entrees, by the way, include salad and dessert.
3. Introductory phrase. To make the deadline, you must apply online.
4. Independent clauses. Mike praised his iPod, but Lisa preferred her BlackBerry.
5. Contrasting statement. It was Marcus, not Ally, who knew how to get to the conference.

Exercise D
1. (2) think, Dr. Simanek,
2. (3) Chicago, Illinois,   6:05 p.m.,
3. (3) International, 1050 Caribbean Way, Miami,
4. (4) October 24, 1901, Annie Taylor, at the age of 64,
5. (4) Rockefeller.,   Oil,   driven, determined,
6. (4) Rockefeller, by the way,   Richland, New York,
7. (3) Minor,   leader,   Worcester,
8. (1) Cambridge,
9. (1) team,
10. (1) article,

11. (3) cubicles, radio, audio,
12. (1) background,
13. C
14. (1) bored,
15. (1) Whatever it is,
16. (4) $2,000,000   equipment, supplies,
17. (2) Cooperation, not competition
18. (2) thing," said Tom Peters,
19. (1) Slingerlands,
20. C

Exercise E
1. b
2. c
3. a
4. b
5. a
6. b
7. c
8. a
9. b
10. a

Chapter 15

LEVEL 1
Exercise B
1. (2) electronically; consequently,
2. (2) arrived, he clocked in,
3. (2) groceries; therefore,
4. (1) world;
5. (10) Cape Town, South Africa; Busan, South Korea; Istanbul, Turkey; Lima, Peru; and Birmingham, Alabama,
6. (1) soon;
7. (1) France;
8. (1) automobiles;
9. (2) problem, Jennifer offered suggestions,
10. (1) audiences;
11. (1) work;
12. (1) passwords;
13. (1) hackers;
14. (2) into; consequently,
15. C
16. (8) Jack Welch, former CEO, General Electric; Arthur Frommer, Founder, Frommer Travel Guides; and Ellen Tauscher, congresswoman,
17. (3) anytime,   businesses; therefore,
18. (3) social sciences, and history; in addition,
19. (3) individual,   scanners; as a result,
20. (5) Hula Burger, McDonald's; the Betamax, Sony; and Breakfast Mates,

LEVEL 2
Exercise B
1. C
2. (1) said:
3. (1) way:
4. (2) cyclones, typhoons
5. (1) outlet:
6. (1) elements:
7. (1) said:
8. (1) name:
9. (2) assets, liabilities,
10. (6) following: Google Maps, Google Finance, Google News, Gmail, Google Health,
11. (3) products: YouTube, Blogger
12. C
13. C
14. (4) sections: introduction, body, summary,
15. C
16. (1) said:
17. (1) these:
18. (1) rules:
19. (1) mistake:
20. (1) said:

Exercise C
Answers will vary.
1. E-mail is used extensively in business today; therefore, the messages I send must be professional.
2. At work I use e-mail for business purposes only; at home I use it to write to my family and friends.
3. I would like to travel to Shanghai, China; Athens, Greece; Budapest, Hungary; and Bangkok, Thailand.
4. Good e-mail messages should have the following traits: clarity, conciseness, and correct form.
5. I have one goal for taking this course: I want to improve my professional writing skills.

LEVEL 3
Exercise B
1. (4) associate; for example, good communication skills, outgoing personality,
2. (3) expertise, administrator; skills,
3. (1) *Burger*:
4. (4) factors; for example, regulatory environment, cultural differences,
5. (2) China; that is,
6. (5) interviews: Thursday at 6:30 p.m., Friday at 3:30 p.m.,
7. (2) monopoly, namely,
8. (2) communications; however,

9. (8) Richard Anderson, CEO, Delta Airlines; Keith Wandell, CEO, Harley Davidson; and Constance Lau, CEO,
10. (3) families: computer equipment, Internet access,

Exercise C
1. b
2. a
3. a
4. a
5. b
6. b
7. a
8. b
9. a
10. b

Chapter 16
LEVEL 1
Exercise B
1. b
2. c
3. a
4. c
5. a
6. a
7. b
8. b
9. b
10. a

Exercise C
1. (5) Susan B. Smith, PhD,   Washington, DC.
2. (4) 9 a.m. until 4 p.m.
3. (3) Dr. Jacqueline A.   2014.
4. (2) requested, didn't you?
5. (3) Soltani, MS,   FDA.
6. (1) created!
7. (2) Stop!   apple!
8. (7) Ms. C. M. Gigliotti   6 p.m., EST.
9. (2) rates,   interested.
10. (1) ESPN!
11. (1) degree.
12. (2) UCLA,   MBA.
13. (4) Ms. J. S.   AFL-CIO.
14. (5) e.g.   i.e.   messages?
15. (2) UK,   USA.
16. (1) current.
17. (2) $45.95   account?
18. (6) individuals: Dr. Lyn Clark, Ms. Frances Hendricks, and Professor Jean Sturgill.
19. (6) Lt. Gen.   U.S.   6 p.m.
20. (3) Well,   job, didn't we?

LEVEL 2
Exercise B
1. b
2. a
3. b
4. a
5. a
6. a
7. b
8. a
9. a
10. a
11. a
12. b
13. b
14. a
15. b
16. b
17. b
18. a
19. a
20. b

Exercise C
1. (2) *The 39 Steps* (have you seen the reviews?)
2. (1) –Tim O'Reilly
3. (1) wikis—these
4. (2) companies (Digg, Last.fm, Newsvine, Tagworld, and YouTube)
5. (2) Web 2.0—privacy, overuse, and etiquette—
6. (2) appointment (try to do so before December 30),
7. (2) dates (see Section 12.3 of the original grant):
8. (1) MapCrawl—these
9. (2) ships (Carnival Dream, Celebrity Equinox, Oasis of the Seas, Seabourn Odyssey, and Viking Legend)
10. (2) sixty (60) days.

Exercise D
1. Numerous appeals, all of which come from concerned parents,
2. Numerous appeals (all all of which come from concerned parents)
3. Numerous appeals—all of which come from concerned parents—

Explanation: Commas setting off the parenthetical element are normal punctuation. Parentheses de-emphasize the element. Dashes emphasize the element.

LEVEL 3
Exercise B
1. The graduating class of '99 held its ten-year reunion on a cruise ship.
2. In three countries (Ukraine, Russia, and Indonesia) over 60 percent of men smoke cigarettes.
3. Smoking is still allowed in Russia's trains, clubs, and restaurants.
4. Louis Camilleri, CEO of Philip Morris, said, "We're being very socially responsible in a rather controversial industry."
5. "Whether you think you can or think you can't," said Henry Ford, "you're right."
6. The word *mashup* is a technology term that is defined as "a Web site that uses content from more than one source to create a completely new service."

7. Kym Anderson's chapter titled "Subsidies and Trade Barriers" appears in the book *How to Spend $50 Billion to Make the World a Better Place.*
8. Did Donald Trump really say, "Anyone who thinks my story is anywhere near over is sadly mistaken"?
9. In his speech the software billionaire said, "Our goal is to link the world irregardless [*sic*] of national boundaries and restrictions."
10. Oprah Winfrey said that the best jobs are those we'd do even if we didn't get paid.
11. Garth said he was "stoked" about his upcoming vacation to Mexico.
12. The postal worker said, "Shall I stamp your package 'Fragile'?"
13. Did you see the article titled "Why Jobs Are Going Unfilled Amid Layoffs" in *BusinessWeek*?
14. The French expression *répondez s'il vous plait* means "respond if you please."
15. Would you please send a current catalog to Globex, Inc.
16. "The man who does not read good books," said Mark Twain, "has no advantage over the man who cannot read them."
17. Three of the largest manufacturers—Dell, IBM, and Hewlett-Packard—submitted bids.
18. In *Forbes* I saw an article titled "Are There Any Rules in the Bailout Game?"
19. Albert Einstein once said that only two things (the universe and human stupidity) are infinite.
20. Albert Einstein once said that only two things—the universe and human stupidity—are infinite.

Exercise C
Answers will vary.

Exercise D
1. b
2. b
3. a
4. b
5. b
6. a
7. c
8. a
9. a
10. c

Chapter 17

LEVEL 1
Exercise B
1. (4) I   Freudian   I   meeting
2. (3) post office   city
3. (2) Internet   online
4. (6) Beaverton, Oregon   Earth Class Mail   technology
5. (4) mail fraud   identity theft
6. (6) United States Postal Service   digital mail
7. (4) family   winter   Sunshine State
8. (5) City   months   April   May   summer

Complete Student Key

9. (7) company employees associate's bachelor's degrees colleges universities
10. (2) students degrees
11. (9) Kansas City Chouteau Room Hyatt Regency Crown Center spring
12. (3) November Veterans Day
13. (6) fall The Prudential Life Insurance Company
14. (5) Green Bay Packers Super Bowl
15. (3) Socratic business management
16. (3) State City Building
17. (3) master's degree UCLA
18. (9) Sierra Club Endangered Species Act gray wolf Northern Rockies
19. (2) Greek engineering
20. (10) hip-hop music Lincoln Navigator DVD TV Sony PlayStation

LEVEL 2
Exercise B
1. (7) federal judge San Francisco businesses Web blind
2. (3) government agencies sites
3. (6) District Judge class-action lawsuit Corporation
4. (3) Minister country TV
5. (6) Uncle Ford Escape West Coast summer
6. (7) Brazil Australia Argentina Southern Hemisphere summers winters
7. (1) Minnesota
8. (5) federal line 7 page 6 Supplement No. 4
9. (4) founders Gate 16 Flight 263 North
10. (2) father *of*
11. (4) Corporation Avenue Vernon California
12. (4) New Regulation in Effect Immediately
13. (5) Googol angel investor Inc. company's
14. (3) federal holiday banks
15. (5) Center Department of Health and Social Services
16. (3) cybercriminals phishing victims
17. (4) Big Mac Coca-Cola
18. (3) Midwesterner south winter
19. (3) northern War Arabica
20. (4) Customer Service Department computer

LEVEL 3
Exercise B
1. (2) planet Pluto
2. (1) It's
3. (9) sun former Vice President graduation address Brigham Young University
4. (1) Yes
5. (2) world's Never
6. (6) English Asians Hong Kong British American
7. (4) Accounting Department invoice Paid

8. (6) minutes   The Vice President   President   Far
9. (3) office manager   regards
10. (7) Cybersecurity   Forensic   Genetic   Geriatric   Health   Homeland   Life

Exercise C
1. a
2. b
3. b
4. a
5. a
6. b
7. b
8. a
9. a
10. b
11. b
12. a
13. a
14. b
15. a
16. b
17. b
18. b
19. a
20. b

Exercise D
Answers will vary.

Exercise E
1. b
2. b
3. a
4. b
5. a
6. b
7. b
8. a
9. a
10. b

Chapter 18

LEVEL 1
Exercise B
1. 17 new status updates
2. C
3. charged 10 cents per copy
4. received four e-mail messages
5. on April 9
6. located on First Street
7. charges of $3.68, $.79, and $40
8. on the 11th of May
9. meeting at 11 a.m.
10. arrived at 10 p.m.
11. a total of 79 orders
12. on August 31
13. C
14. costs $49
15. Twenty-seven interviewees
16. 1,319 people visited
17. C
18. One Hampton Square
19. has 66 rooms
20. at 18:00
21. on 15 April 2009
22. 2742 Eighth Street
23. 5:30 p.m.
24. call (800) 123-4567
25. for $100
26. costs exactly 90 cents
27. at 18307 11th Street
28. call (800) 598-3459
29. C
30. bought two lattes

Complete Student Key 37

Exercise C
1. A total of 259 identity theft complaints were filed with the FTC on November 2 alone.
2. Please call me at (925) 685-1230, Ext. 309.
3. On April 15 Alicia submitted the following petty cash disbursements: $2.80, $.95, $5, and $.25.
4. Erika Rothschild moved from 1716 Sunset Drive to One Bellingham Court.
5. Twenty-four different wireless packages are available from our three local dealers.
6. On the 18th of March, I sent you three e-mail messages about restricting Internet use.
7. Although McDonald's advertised a sandwich that cost only 99 cents, most customers found that lunch cost between $3 and $3.99.
8. Regular work breaks are scheduled at 10 a.m. and again at 3:30 p.m.
9. We want to continue operations through the 30th, but we may be forced to close by the 22nd.
10. The United States experienced 20,000 job cuts between April 1 and April 30.

LEVEL 2
Exercise B
1. 5, 1,680
2. Number 4, 25
3. 3, 4, 8
4. 6-month
5. 16
6. 825 million
7. numbers
8. 8400
9. 53 million
10. 10, 8
11. 41, 33
12. 44, 2, $74 billion
13. 90
14. 800,000
15. 2
16. twenty-four
17. 2 years 6 months
18. 24, 20, 100
19. seven years, $50 million
20. 21.5 million

Exercise C
1. sold for $1.5 million
2. 107 5-page essays
3. a law that is 1 year 2 months and 5 days old
4. nine offices with 11 computers and 15 desks
5. three 75-pound weights
6. loan period of 60 days
7. Joan Brault, 74, and Frank Brault, 72
8. 8 Account No. 362486012
9. $5.8 billion
10. Highway 29
11. you are No. 25
12. 59 employee suggestions
13. C or about 300 voters
14. 4.4 million people
15. Section 3.2
16. nine 3-bedroom apartments
17. warranty period of 2 years (business term)

18. C
19. selected Nos. 305 and 409
20. took out a 9-month CD (business term)

LEVEL 3
Exercise B
1. "Kingda Ka," which claims to be the world's fastest and tallest roller coaster, travels 128 miles per hour and is 456 feet high.
2. When the ride first opened on May 21, 2005, nearly one third of the visitors to Six Flags Great Adventure in New Jersey lined up for a high-speed joyride on four 18-passenger rail cars.
3. Swiss engineers used precise instruments to ensure that Kingda Ka's 3,118 feet of steel track were within 0.05 inches of specifications.
4. To ride Kingda Ka, you must be at least 54 inches tall but less than 6 feet 5 inches tall.
5. Only the Kingda Ka ride can reach speeds of 128 miles per hour in 3.3 seconds, achieving a negative gravity force with 6.5 seconds of weightlessness at the top before taking a 41-story plunge.
6. Located in the Fourth Congressional District, Six Flags Great Adventure is 74 miles from New York City and attracts over 3 million visitors each summer.
7. The square mileage of Washington, DC, is 68.2; and its population is about 550,000.
8. Although Washington, DC, which has a population of 591,833, its population during the week grows to one million because of commuters.
9. African Americans make up approximately 55.6 percent of the population in Washington, DC.
10. Almost two thirds of eligible Americans voted in the last presidential election.

Exercise C
Answers will vary.

Exercise D
1. a
2. a
3. b
4. a
5. b
6. a
7. a
8. a
9. c
10. b